FREE
ANA

Members of the Rebe. ۔.., ͻle to
give talks to anyone interested in Anarcııⱋıͷ.

Maybe you teach A-level politics?

We are familiar with the Edexcel and AQA curriculums used by most
schools and are happy to come and talk about Anarchism or use
Anarchist ideas to illustrate other parts of the curriculum.

Maybe you teach younger children?

We are happy to come into school and take an assembly on non-
hierarchical ways of working and living.

Maybe you work in FE?

or run a local group and would like someone to come and provide your
students or your group with an introduction to Anarchism, or a talk on
Anarchism and Religion.

We are happy to work round the requirements of a curriculum or to
conduct more free ranging interactive sessions. We work in pairs and
have already undertaken sessions with sixth formers in London schools
and given talks to groups across a diverse range of settings. Students
and attendees have found the sessions engaging and informative and
there has been a real buzz, with participants eager to interact, ask
questions and contribute.

If you, your school, or your group are interested in hosting a
talk, please get in touch.

Contact Jane
a_levelpoliticsanarchism@yahoo.co.uk

Putting this booklet together was a truly collective effort.

Rebel City Collective would like to thank all our friends, comrades and families who contributed with answers to questions, comments, criticisms, editing, proofreading and ideas. Your support was invaluable.

Lastly, thanks to the many students across the UK who asked the questions this booklet was based on, when we visited your school, FE college or university, to discuss with you what anarchism is all about.

1st edition published Summer 2023

By Rebel City – **www.rebelcitylondon.wordpress.com**

A catalogue record for this book is available from the British Library

ISBN 978-0-9537390-2-8

This book is dedicated to all those worldwide fighting for an anarchist society

Written and designed by members of Rebel City and friends

Distributed by:

AK Press, 33 Tower Street, Edinburgh, EH6 7BN - akedinburgh@gmail.com

PM Press – info@pmpress.org.uk

For more copies of this book contact either of the distributors or Rebel City at:

londonrebelcity@gmail.com

Contents

themselves or others? Would treatment be compulsory?

16   How would you deal with antisocial behaviour, bullying and crime to keep people safe?

17   What about murderers, rapists and paedophiles?

18   So you would get rid of prisons and the police then? How would that work?

19   How do we distribute resources fairly?

20   Would there be money in an anarchist society?

21   Without money, how would we trade and exchange goods and services?

22   Without money, what would motivate people to work, or encourage creativity and innovation?

23   Would people be able to have property?

24   What would stop individuals/groups taking or hoarding resources?

25   What if no-one wanted to do unpleasant tasks?

26   So what about people who don't want to work at all?

27   What about people who aren't able to speak for themselves, because of age, illness or disability?

28   What about identity politics? What if different groups feel their rights are in conflict? How would conflict and discord be dealt with?

29   Do anarchists believe in free speech?

30   Would religion have a place in an anarchist society?

31   Would children and young people have a say in deciding how society is run?

32   How would education work?

33   How would you deal with the climate and environmental crises?

34   Would anarchists ban scientific research and technology development?

35   Would we still have nuclear families in an anarchist society?

36   Would drugs be allowed? What about alcohol and tobacco?

37   Would media/social media be regulated?

38   What will happen to fashion, art, music, culture, entertainment fun?

HOW WE GET FROM HERE TO THERE?

39   But don't we need political parties and leaders to be able to make changes?

40   Shouldn't we gradually reform what we have rather than changing everything?

41   What is this direct action you lot talk about?

42   Would a revolution be violent? Wouldn't governments suppress any attempts at real change with force?

43   How do we know a revolution won't end in chaos and destruction?

44   Why would anyone support some sort of revolution when the outcome is unknown?

45   What would happen to people who opposed an anarchist revolution?

46   Isn't it "human nature" to compete with others to get the best for us and our families?

47   Don't most people want an easy life and are happy for others to make decisions?

48   How do we get the rich to give up their wealth?

49   What about power? How do we get them to share that?

50   Does the revolution need to happen globally or can it happen on a smaller scale?

51   Can we really change things?

52   So ask yourself, what kind of future do I want to see for myself and the world?

1 Introduction

This booklet has been put together by Rebel City, a London-based anarchist group.

We publish newsletters and pamphlets on community organisation and anarchism and we visit schools and colleges to talk to young people about our ideas.

During discussions with students many questions arise so we decided to compile a booklet answering some of those questions. Answers have been contributed by many different people and will, we hope, provide a straightforward but varied account of how we can create a better society by organising ourselves according to anarchist principles.

The booklet is divided into three sections. The first, "What is anarchism?" describes the basic ideas of anarchism and how they differ from other systems. The second section, "What would an anarchist society look like?" shows how those principles might be applied in different parts of society. The third section is titled "How do we get from here to there?". This is a question for everybody - How do we start organising ourselves now, so that we can truly create a better world?

We have included a glossary of words mentioned in the text and highlighted in **bold** throughout the booklet.

2 The state we are in

Before we talk about anarchism, let's look where we are at the moment. In the UK, and most of the world, we have huge levels of poverty. Millions die from illnesses which are curable with medicines that cost pennies while others have multiple yachts and homes that are eye-wateringly expensive.

Throughout the world racism and sexism is widespread. Large numbers of people are killed or attacked because of their colour, sex, sexuality or gender. In the UK millions are forced to use food banks and worldwide millions die from starvation. At the same time food rots in the ground because it's better for big businesses' profits to let it rot rather than feed people dying due to lack of food. People in the UK are choosing between heating or eating (and sometimes can't afford either). Over 30% of the world's population suffered food insecurity in 2020 and it's getting worse (World Economic Forum tinyurl.com/3mkenvzy)

We are destroying the environment, yet multinational corporations dig up more and more of our natural resources to make more and more products we don't need. We pump tons of pollution into the environment causing global warming and destroying our children's and our own health. Our healthcare and education systems are in ruins due to lack of funds. Yet the super-rich spend billions launching rockets into space so they can have a better holiday than the rest of us.

Capitalism and **state run socialism** are failing the vast majority of us to the point where they destroy our health and kill millions of us. We believe this is just wrong. It benefits a very tiny minority while billions of us struggle.

How is this right? Why do we put up with it? Are billions of us being conned into accepting poverty as something we feel we can't change?

The present system is corrupt, built for the wealthy and downright wrong. There is a better system. And we feel that's anarchism.

WHAT IS ANARCHISM?

see glossary near the back of the booklet for meaning of words in bold

3   So what is anarchism?

We are all brought up and educated in a society of bosses, profits, landlords and the division between rich and poor. This is **capitalism**. We know how the system works, know our place in society and what's expected of us. But what about anarchism? How would an anarchist society work?

Anarchists believe society should be based on three principles: freedom, equality, and **solidarity** (supporting each other). To develop fully, anarchists believe that people must be free. Genuine freedom can only be achieved in societies based on voluntary association rather than force, and in societies where everyone is equal. No real freedom can exist in societies divided by **class** and with gross inequalities in power, wealth, and privilege.

Solidarity and **mutual aid**, are where we support each other when needed, without asking for anything in return. It also means treating everyone as equals and creating relationships and structures that support freedom for all.

anarchists believe society should be based on three principles: freedom, equality, and solidarity

Structures will be **accountable**. This means having to answer for your actions and decisions to others connected to you – workmates, neighbours, etc. Decisions flow from the bottom up, skills, resources and information are shared, and tasks are rotated. In an anarchist society people won't be bullied into doing anything by threats or be forced to work by fear of poverty.

4   But isn't anarchism all about chaos and disorder?

No! This is a common error when we talk to people about anarchism. And one the **state** and the media deliberately use to make anarchism less appealing to people

Anarchists reject the state, power, superiority and **hierarchy** and would argue that the world is already in chaos and disorder because of the systems put in place by the state and those with power.

Look at the world we live in: for hundreds of years, half of the population have been living in poverty. Even though there is more than enough for everyone, people have starved to death, become homeless, lacked life-saving medicines, endured racism and fought wars for the benefit of the rich and powerful.

Today we face climate change extinction, a real threat brought about by the greed and incompetence of our so called leaders. If all this isn't chaos and disorder, what is?

Anarchists would replace the harmful systems in place today with **collective** organising. Everybody will have an opportunity to discuss and be part of the decision making process on anything that is important to them.

How does this work? Read on for some ideas how anarchism can lead to a more equal society, where we share the world's wealth and resources to make a more harmonious world.

the world is already in chaos and disorder

see glossary near the back of the booklet for meaning of words in bold

POPULAR
MISCONCEPTION
OF A TYPICAL
ANARCHIST

ACTUAL
ANARCHISTS
IN REAL
LIFE

5   So Anarchists believe in democracy?

If by democracy you mean the present set up, sometimes referred to as **representative democracy**, then no. Here, you're allowed to vote every four or five years for a narrow selection of candidates who are meant to represent you. In fact politicians mainly represent the ruling class and they're totally un**accountable** and regularly break their election promises.

If you mean **direct democracy**, then yes. Here, **assemblies**, which everyone can go to, decide on their **collective** view including actions that should be taken. These assemblies send people (**delegates**) to put that view across at larger assemblies.

So decisions are made "bottom up" (from the people) not "top down" (from elected politicians). Delegates are not in a position of power as we feel power corrupts. If a delegate doesn't represent your assembly correctly, they can be instantly **recalled** (replaced by someone else there and then).

In an anarchist society all decisions would be made as close as possible to those most affected, so we would see local neighbourhood and workplace assemblies as the place where the main decisions are made. These would then come together with neighbouring areas and workplaces over a larger area so everyone truly has a say in the decision making. So you would regularly go to your local assembly where you would discuss everything from bin collection to huge global issues. You would also sometimes go to other assemblies to tell them what your assembly had decided.

if by democracy you mean the present set up, then no. if you mean direct democracy, then yes

6   What is self-organisation/ non-hierarchical organisation and why is it important to anarchism?

Present society seems to think we need leaders and rulers, but this is a lie promoted by those same leaders and rulers.

Self and **non-hierarchical** organising is where there is no leader, president or manager type role and no lesser roles either. Instead, members of a group, organisation or **collective** (a group of people working together) all have an equal say in how the group is run, what the aims are and how to reach them. Self-organisation can be applied to all sorts of groups: e.g. a local food co-op, where a group of people get together and buy food in bulk and share it between them, or workers kicking out their bosses and running their factories themselves.

Even though there might be specialist roles, no one's role is more important than any other, as every job is essential for the group to run properly. Many non-hierarchical organisations try to rotate roles so that people only remain in place for a fixed time before handing the role over

see glossary near the back of the booklet for meaning of words in bold

to someone else. This means many people develop the skills, knowledge and experience to keep things running smoothly. And it's one way to prevent anyone becoming irreplaceable. Once someone - or some group - is more important than anyone else you're on the way from leaders to rulers, and back to the oppression and exploitation we want to end.

Discussions about how the group operates are decided in an **assembly** or group meeting where everybody involved is welcome and has an equal say. Decisions are usually made by **consensus** so everyone has a fair say in how things are run and the workload is shared. It also means that the people doing the work have a say in how the organisation is managed and encourages collective responsibility and ownership of the outcome.

With controversial or urgent issues, different groups may have different guidelines that allow them to make decisions without full consensus. But these guidelines would be made at the beginning and with everyone's agreement. This way everyone in a group or workplace has a say in how these issues will be decided well in advance of them arising.

For more information and a real world example look up tinyurl.com/589evzyu

wherever working people have fought for themselves, anarchists have supported them

in Spain workers ran factories, transport and food distribution

7 What have anarchists done for society?

In times of conflict, anarchists put their ideas into practice. They take part in creating and defending workers' struggles which include factory and land occupations. They also help supply food, housing, health care and other necessities. Looking back in history, anarchists were hugely active in the **Paris Commune** Uprisings in 1871; Revolutions in **Russia** in 1905 and 1917, Germany and Hungary in 1918, **Spain** in 1936 and Hungary in 1956.

Three explicitly anarchist events were:
- **Ukraine** 1917 to 1921, with land occupations and redistribution, and peasant-run soviets.
- **Manchuria's Anarchist zone** 1929-31, in what is now North East China, had shops where everything was free, worker and peasant **cooperatives**. Schools were set up throughout their territories, along with Regional **assemblies**.
- **Spain 1936**, workers ran factories, transport and food distribution particularly in Catalonia. In the countryside peasants took over and organised the land and shared what they

2

see glossary near the back of the booklet for meaning of words in bold

produced **collectively**, passing their surplus on to the cities. All these offer glimpses of what a new society could look like.

Today, things like **housing and workers' co-ops** are good examples of direct democracy. Those living together or workers in a workplace are the ones who make all the decisions.

Non-hierarchical decision making has come out of anarchist ways of organising and is where everyone is equally involved in making the decisions. These practices are now all in common use. Anarchists have also explored how and when it's better to use **consensus decision making** (where everyone needs to agree before a decision can be made) rather than simple majority voting.

Wherever and however working people have fought for themselves, anarchists have supported them, without taking over or trying to lead.

people are perfectly capable of organising society themselves without leaders

"We are convinced that liberty without socialism is privilege and injustice; and that socialism without liberty is slavery and brutality"

~ Mikhail Bakunin ~

8 What's the difference between anarchism and socialism?

Anarchism, **socialism** and **communism** are similar in many ways. In fact, originally there was no difference between them. They all grew out of the workers' movement of the late 19th century which aimed to create a society different from the existing **capitalism**. The aim was to build a society in which everything would be held in common and everyone equal, sharing out the products of their labour.

Differences developed in the late 19th and early 20th centuries leading to different political views. One was **authoritarian socialism/communism** and the other **libertarian communism/ socialism**, the latter often referred to simply as anarchism. Anarchists believe revolution will happen when people come together and organise society for the benefit of all. This will totally change society to one where we all have what we need and will destroy capitalism in the process. People are perfectly capable of organising society themselves, without leaders.

Authoritarian socialists and communists believe change is only possible with the right leadership - namely them!

3

see glossary near the back of the booklet for meaning of words in bold

WHAT WOULD AN ANARCHIST SOCIETY LOOK LIKE?

4

see glossary near the back of the booklet for meaning of words in bold

9 How would anarchists organise locally, nationally, globally to get things done?

As mentioned in section 6, anarchists' preferred ways of organising are **self-organisation** or **non-hierarchical** organising. Another term we sometimes use is **participatory democracy**. We have also mentioned **consensus decision making** before. In all of these, everyone affected has a fair say and decisions are made by everyone involved.

As for actually organising, one way could be as follows: each street or estate has an **assembly** which makes decisions for that street or estate. A number of these near each other then come together and make decisions for a wider area. Not everyone could, or would want to go, so each street/estate selects a **delegate** to represent them. Each area also selects a delegate for a larger area meeting (these meetings could use electronic communication tools if face to face isn't practical), and so on until you are at (what we presently call) national or international levels.

Likewise, each workplace, shop, community centre or group, would also make decisions affecting them. Let's take a community centre. The workers here would make decisions on how it's run. They would also meet with other community centres locally, and possibly nationally and internationally. They would also meet with other workplaces, shops, and street assemblies, to see what they needed from the community centre, and vice versa.

This sort of happens today – it's just the ruling class making these decisions and we don't have a say.

There are many other ways we could organise in an anarchist society. The above is just one possible example.

10 Oh! So there wouldn't be countries then?

Indeed not!

Borders are just lines drawn on the world map to separate countries and throughout history these change depending on who's in power. Borders have changed many times as one leader grabs land from another, generally by force. These borders are often cruel, as families and whole communities get split up and separated into different countries.

Borders are useful for those in power as separate rulers make laws to oppress ordinary people inside "their country". It's also useful for the rulers as they convince ordinary people to support them, claiming we are all part of the same "country". This breeds **nationalism** as we are conned to believe we are different and superior to people from another country. Often this leads to conflict and war.

We are not saying there shouldn't be different languages, customs and traditions that we all grew up with. In fact, without borders and separate countries, it will be easier for people to decide how they want to mix and with whom. Also without leaders and countries, people would be able to keep their

see glossary near the back of the booklet for meaning of words in bold

local traditions – unlike in many parts of the world today where local languages and customs are banned and the nation's rules are imposed on you.

We have one planet, and anarchists don't agree it should be divided up into small bits and that you can only live where you are told. Anarchists believe people should be able to move freely throughout the world and live wherever they want to without countries and their borders,

You should also be able to love and live with whoever you want to, This is often impossible when you have countries, as you generally have to live in your "own" country and abide by its rules.

we have one planet, and anarchists don't agree it should be divided

11 Will people/communities be able to keep national or cultural identities and customs?

Anarchists don't agree with national identities or borders as we feel this leads to conflict, power relationships and divides us all along false lines. After all, most nations were created by wars, land grabs and lines drawn on maps at international conferences by the rich and powerful for their own benefit. "I am British" (for example) doesn't really mean much to us and in the present climate leaves many people feeling like they don't belong. Why would anyone want that?

Under anarchism, with national borders a thing of the past, we would expect people to travel and set up home anywhere in the world they wished. We would hope everyone would see themselves as part of the "human race" not British, Cuban, Nigerian or any other nationality.

Cultural identities and customs can be different. These are something we have all grown up with over generations and keep histories alive. As long as they are not oppressive and don't exploit anyone, we see no reason why these shouldn't continue.

But at the end of the day it would be for every area to decide what they want for themselves. However, if they imposed oppressive customs, we expect people would just leave and move to an area where they felt they fitted in better, or stay and argue why the oppressive customs need to stop.

we do all this now. all we are suggesting is we just do it without some boss breathing down our necks

12 How do you run large industries like power and food distribution without bosses?

Although it doesn't seem like it, most of the time large industries are run by workers anyway, in that we do most of the work. It's just that presently the bosses' jobs are seen as more important. And they get paid massively more. Those at the top get all the credit when in fact hundreds of people make the organisation work smoothly. Hospitals, local authorities, transport and, yes, power industries and food distribution are run best when the workers are in control. Bosses can actually make things worse as they think more about profits for themselves than what's good for society.

One way power production and distribution could be organised is that each workplace has its own **factory committees/groups**, where everyone there is involved in the decision making. Local people, who don't work in the factory, might also have a say on behalf of the local community on some issues. The workers might then come together with other factories on a larger scale, but still fairly local area, to decide on the needs of that area.

These local groups could then join together nationally (and internationally) to manage production, supply and distribution. This would ensure each area had enough of what was needed.

There would be people chosen by their workmates who would work with people in similar factories in all the other areas. But there would also be people who work with other types of industry and local community organisations in the local area, so supply and distribution could be organised properly locally as well.

Let's remember – we actually do all this now. All we are suggesting is we just do it without some boss breathing down our necks.

see glossary near the back of the booklet for meaning of words in bold

13 How would people be housed?

Presently, many of us live in homes that are too small, or in a terrible state of repair. Most of us worry about how we'll pay our rent or mortgage and if we might lose our home. Thousands of us are homeless or living in temporary housing. Meanwhile landlords are using this as a get rich quick scheme. Some people have second or even third homes. Houses are left empty as an investment or rented out as holiday lets or Airbnbs for even greater profits.

In an anarchist society all housing would be used for homes, not for making money. Everyone would have a good quality, warm, secure home with enough space for all their family.

In the short term, we could start by taking the empty homes, second homes, holiday homes and Airbnbs and giving them to people who

need them. We could take the huge mansions some people have and use them for large families or **housing co-ops** (where people organise their housing needs collectively).

Longer term, housing would be communally owned. Every estate or street could have its own **assembly** where everyone living there has a say in how housing is shared out. Maybe all the streets in an area would meet to support each other and plan on a bigger scale for repairs and new house building. There could be a website where we swap homes if we want to live in a different area or need a different size home.

These are just some ideas. There are so many better ways to organise housing than the corrupt system we have now, where profit comes before people's needs.

How would *you* make sure everyone had a good home?

14 How would an effective healthcare system be run under anarchism?

In an anarchist society looking after ourselves and each other would form the basis of our society. People generally want to learn skills which allow them to feed and shelter themselves and look after their own health, and an anarchist society would facilitate this.

conditions associated with poverty and deprivation would be greatly reduced

see glossary near the back of the booklet for meaning of words in bold

Democratic community health **collectives** (a group of people working together) including trained doctors and nurses could share medical knowledge and nursing skills throughout the community. Everyone could learn first aid and how to treat some illnesses and injuries themselves, and safely use accessible resources (such as herbs and medicines), as part of their education and ongoing workplace training.

Good health is also based on good nutrition. Communities would be producing food not for profit but to provide themselves with healthy, sustainable diets, and this would likely result in a reduction in many preventable conditions such as diabetes, heart disease and dental problems. Many conditions associated with poverty and deprivation would be greatly reduced.

Communities would decide what medical facilities, research and training to use resources on, depending on their local needs.

When people are well-informed they can decide with their medical collectives what treatments are best for them. With community training and support, good nutrition, improved social fabric, and less pollution, mental and physical health would improve.

6

15 But how would you deal with people in mental health crises who may be a danger to themselves or others? Would treatment be compulsory?

Yes, a community might decide that compulsory treatment be allowed, but it would be taken much more seriously and be much more transparent.

How would you like to be treated if you were having a mental health crisis and people around you were afraid you might harm yourself or them? Would you be prepared to temporarily give up some of your freedom? To get the support and care you require to recover from these urges to behave in a harmful way?

Or would you want to be allowed to harm yourself or others? Would you expect to be held responsible for your behaviour if no-one tried to stop or support you?

And if you were temporarily restricting someone's else's freedom (either by physical restraint or heavy medication) how could you do this in an **accountable** and fair way?

How do we ensure that this restriction of freedom does not in itself become harmful?

People who harm others or themselves are often ashamed after the event. This shame can actually compound existing mental health concerns, thereby potentially leading to more harmful behaviour. So it's in our mutual interest to support people as much as possible to prevent harmful acts and help them recover afterwards. This means acting in **solidarity** with the person and trying to understand what led to the mental health crisis and working together to create circumstances where the person can thrive. It's important to remember - the person experiencing the crisis may also teach us things about the circumstances in which they, and us, are living as mental health crises don't come out of nowhere.

16 How would you deal with antisocial behaviour, bullying and crime to keep people safe?

If you think of a time you wanted to, or did, behave antisocially, what stopped you? And if you think of a time someone was behaving antisocially towards you, what would have made you feel safe?

Whether it's in this society or an anarchist one, if we collectively decide that it is okay to temporarily limit a person's freedom so they can't continue behaving antisocially, what ensures the **accountability** of the people doing the limiting? If it was you whose freedom was being limited, what would make you feel it was fair? And what kind of support should we provide to the person who has suffered?

To deal with antisocial behaviour there are many ideas for **'alternative' justice**, where everyone affected by the antisocial behaviour works together to address it. With **restorative**

see glossary near the back of the booklet for meaning of words in bold

justice, alleged offenders have to admit their guilt and try to make up for it. **Transformative justice** aims to change society as a whole as well as the individuals involved. It tries to find out why the person was victimised, provides support to them, and demands the offender work to change themselves. This ties in with the idea of 'circles of support', where people who have behaved in antisocial ways by committing acts of violence receive intense support AND are expected to develop the skills to address any urges to commit such acts again.

Different communities in an anarchist society might well try out varying versions of these - or experiment with others!

a society run on anarchist principles would likely have much lower levels of violence

17 What about murderers, rapists and paedophiles?

To solve a problem, it helps to know the cause. What causes people to murder, rape, or abuse children?

Many studies show the greater the economic inequality the more violent a society. Childhood neglect, abuse, poverty and deprivation can contribute to aggressive behaviour. So can substance abuse, physical and psychological trauma and mental health issues. (tinyurl.com/yc3bkvxs)

A society run on anarchist principles, without economic inequalities, would likely have much lower levels of violence.

Lifelong accessible education, including psychological support and emotional education from an early age, voluntary employment according to interest and ability, and decent collective responsibility for childhood nurturing, proper care for people with mental health issues, and community support for those tackling drug and alcohol issues; all of these would address many of the causes of violent crime.

Rape and sexual aggression arise from the need to dominate and have power over those weaker or more vulnerable. Perpetrators often witnessed or experienced abuse themselves and repeat the abuse. Everyone having an equal voice, and control over their lives and their bodies, can prevent people being controlled and abused. Rehabilitation and psychological support for offenders and survivors helps break cycles of abuse.

Even when we address the economic and social inequalities, there may still be individuals who are a danger to others. We don't have all the answers and in future, communities may need to try different approaches. Sometimes dangerous people may need to be supported in ways where they can't harm others. However, we believe that most violent crimes are due to inequality, deprivation or social, medical or psychological issues. Once those have been addressed, as they would in an anarchist society, the likelihood is that persistently violent or dangerous people would be a rarity.

there are many ideas for 'alternative' justice

UNTIL ALL ARE FREE, NO ONE IS FREE.

no cages.
no prisons.
no borders.

see glossary near the back of the booklet for meaning of words in bold

18 So you would get rid of prisons and the police then? How would that work?

Anarchists feel a future society would be much better without them.

The best police do is to arrest someone after the event, they rarely stop it. They are also not much of a deterrent to illegal activities. We are being conned by the police, **state** and corporate media into thinking they are a vital part of our communities.

Many people in prison are there for crimes of poverty (theft, shoplifting, drugs, etc.).

SEE NO EVIL   SPEAK NO EVIL   HEAR NO EVIL

The police, prisons and courts are arms of the state, and are there to keep the state safe. They are generally used AGAINST ordinary people – not for them. They have been likened to an 'army of occupation'. And even when they seem to help us (like catching a murderer) it's because the state needs us to believe in them – it's not for our benefit.

An anarchist society wouldn't have money or poverty so the vast majority of crime will disappear. With strong communities supporting each other, people won't feel alienated, will know others around them and be less likely to harm and rob each other.

When a dispute breaks out, local communities would get involved before it got serious. All those involved, and members of the community, would discuss their issues together and try and come to an agreement they all find acceptable. Everything will be open, transparent and controlled by us all.

People who might be a danger to others could be supported in their own homes or maybe a community house. The aim would be to give them the help and support they need to bring them back into general society as soon as they are no longer a threat, with ongoing support where necessary.

from each according to ability, to each according to need

19 How do we distribute resources fairly?

In present day **capitalist** society, **scarcity** is often deliberate to benefit the **ruling class**. Some examples are leaving 'excess' crops unharvested, or leaving food stocks in storage, or actually destroying them, to keep profits high.

When people think of rationing they often think about during World War 2 when the amount of

we will collectively decide what we all need and then freely produce it between us all

many goods including food was restricted. However, rationing still exists now. It's just done by pricing, as large numbers of us can't afford enough food, heating, adequate housing or other things we need. Under capitalism a very small minority live very well and the world's majority live in varying degrees of poverty.

The basis for resource distribution in a future anarchist society is "fairness". Anarchists believe "from each according to their abilities [i.e. work], to each according to their needs". We don't mean everyone has the same amount of food, heating, etc. It's that everyone has what they need to stay fit and healthy and have an enjoyable life. This will vary depending on whether they are a child, adult, elderly, have a disability, are sick/healthy, pregnant etc.

For example, who decides what food a person needs, and how much? Each of us, as part of the community, will have an equal say in what is produced and how, and in deciding how resources

see glossary near the back of the booklet for meaning of words in bold

(peoples' labour etc.) are used to produce the food that each of us needs. When resources are scarce it's crucial all of us are part of deciding how to ration them fairly. This avoids resentment about why some people have more, as we were all part of the decision making process.

20 Would there be money in an anarchist society?

No. Money allows people to hoard resources as individual wealth. The gap between rich and poor then grows ever wider, which causes resentment and divisions in society. It leads to worry and stress, for those without money, which is not good for our well-being and is just downright unfair and unjust.

12

see glossary near the back of the booklet for meaning of words in bold

People then want more and more money and confuse what they want with what they actually need.

For instance, there is a cure for African Sleeping sickness. The same drug gets rid of female facial hair. When the **capitalist** market is faced with saving millions of Africans from a deadly disease or removing female facial hair, it chooses whichever produces most profit/money (removing female facial hair). So, thousands die for the sake of profit.

In today's society a small percentage of people have vast amounts of wealth while more than half the world's population live in poverty. We have enough resources in this world to satisfy everyone's needs. Yet those with money have all the luxuries life offers, while at the other end of the scale people world-wide with little money are barely surviving.

As well as actively getting rid of money, in an anarchist society there will be no need for it either. We will **collectively** decide what we all need and then freely produce it between us all. Everything will then be freely available, so we all take what we need to live. Or, if there isn't enough of something we will share or decide who is in most need of it. These are much fairer ways to distribute our resources than those with most money getting first choice.

Anarchists believe 'from each according toability, to each according to need'. This basically means we all contribute what we can and we all use the resources we each need.

we would just do what needed doing simply because it needed doing

21 Without money, how would we trade and exchange goods and services?

Present **capitalist** society pushes us to buy things we don't need, so capitalists can make more money from us. As an example, we don't need a new phone every year, but most of us buy one. Under anarchism, what we produce would be about what we really need **collectively**. This is not to suggest that life will be basic and without luxuries.

Presently, "trade" means selling something to someone else to make a profit/money. With no money in an anarchist society a lot of "trading" would stop. Things like Britain transporting and selling lamb to Australia and Australia then selling lamb to Britain is environmentally and morally wrong. People will decide what they need and produce these things locally - so goods aren't transported around the world. Further, many things are just not needed in an anarchist society. So huge amounts of "trade" would just stop happening.

22 Without money, what would motivate people to work, or encourage creativity and innovation?

If we did need to exchange goods between different areas, there are many ways this could be done under anarchism. Three examples are:

- Some communities will produce more than they need and give the extra to communities who need it. And likewise get what they need from different communities who have extra.
- It may be that there would be limited amounts of "barter", where you give us something (say food) and we give you something in return (say help mending your computers).
- It could be decided democratically in local **assemblies** where everyone gets an equal say so everyone gets what they need.
- Exchanging goods and services such as food, homes, health care, everything - between communities would be decided by **delegates** of all the relevant communities coming together.

This would happen at a local level but also national level and if needed international level.

So much of our lives now involves money. It almost feels like without it, human activity would stop altogether! But really, money is just one way of managing and controlling the things we do.

Humans existed a long while before money was even thought of. And, before money, people still worked, created art, came up with new ideas, built homes, exchanged goods and provided what people needed to live. In today's society many of us volunteer, support others and do community based work. Two of many examples are lifeboat volunteers and foodbanks. Anarchists believe it would be the same in an anarchist society – but on a much bigger scale.

see glossary near the back of the booklet for meaning of words in bold

Anarchism would get rid of tedious money-making jobs. We would decide the work we did and how and when it happened. We would be free to be creative, to innovate and to plan together. Without having to make and protect the wealth of others, we would have time to be creative and reflective.

Rather than being motivated by money, we would be motivated by supporting each other and knowing our labours benefit us all. Getting a fair share of our efforts, rather than a boss taking all the profits, means people would be motivated. With no money, everything we needed would also be free - we just all need to spend a bit of time helping to produce it. Unchained from making money for bosses and shareholders, imagine what we could create, invent and achieve?

Many things we do as humans are organised without anyone making us or any direct financial motivation. In a society that was free and fun, we wouldn't need to be pushed or bribed, we would just do what needed doing simply because it needed doing.

in an anarchist society there would be enough for everyone

23 Would people be able to have property?

In present society, when we think of property we think of two kinds. One is the workplace the boss owns, the houses the landlord owns, the estates landowners own. The other is whatever we own individually for our personal use - from music to computers to clothes. Down to your toothbrush!

In an anarchist society the first lot would belong to the community, and would be used however that community thought best. In effect they would, in an anarchist society, become communal, **collective** or shared property.

What about stuff for our personal use? Anything society had enough of could be held individually. Rarer items could be kept in a communal space or there could be a register of who had them so others could use them.

In the society we imagine, people wouldn't be competing for resources (including property and other material things). We would expect people to work together and share out what people need. (No buying and selling!). Indeed, the aim is to reach a time when everyone is able to take what they need!

We don't think that people should have more than they reasonably need. With housing for example, when the children have left home and someone has a huge house just for themselves, they could swap with a larger household who need more space.

But, what if they like the extra space and don't want to "downsize"? We're not saying there'd be no conflicts of interest in an anarchist society. But these would be worked through with everyone in that community, group or area. And different communities and groups may collectively agree different solutions to solving these problems!

see glossary near the back of the booklet for meaning of words in bold

24 What would stop individuals/ groups taking or hoarding resources?

Resources are hoarded because people believe there isn't enough to go around. Panic buying in the early days of the Covid pandemic was an example. Some people thought there would be shortages of supplies so they rushed around supermarkets buying up things like toilet paper to last months! Once people realised there wasn't going to be a shortage the hoarding behaviour stopped. However, most people didn't act like this. Many did the opposite and set up **mutual aid** support groups that made sure those less able, or ill, were supported.

An anarchist society would be based on the principles of **solidarity** and mutual aid. People's natural tendencies would be to care for and have empathy with others. Also, there shouldn't be a need to hoard because of the worry that there will be shortages. Under **capitalism**, many resources are used to produce things that we don't need such as weapons and a ridiculous array of unnecessary consumer goods. In an anarchist society, generally there would be enough resources available if we produce what we really need for everyone to live good quality lives.

volunteers for unpleasant tasks could be exempt from other activities or have more time off

see glossary near the back of the booklet for meaning of words in bold

25 What if no one wanted to do unpleasant tasks?

Unpopular jobs will still need to be done. Who does them will have to be worked out by each community. No-one should be forced into doing them.

People might do these jobs because they enjoy doing them and they want to help the community they live in. In a limited way, this presently happens, where **capitalists** can't make a profit from it. For example, people regularly volunteer to do miserable tasks like cleaning beaches after oil spills from ships or dangerous jobs like mine clearing in war zones.

Unpleasant jobs could also be shared on a rota system. Or, if some people volunteered to do them because others didn't want to, then the volunteers could be exempt from other activities if they wished, or have more time off for doing this work.

Technology could play a part too by allowing jobs to become automated. We are already seeing this in today's society. Unlike automation in capitalist society, workers themselves could use automation to assist them, or choose to fully automate particular jobs.

These are just a few thoughts and ideas. There are many more.

26 So what about people who don't want to work at all?

Given that work is voluntary in an anarchist society – nobody would be forced to work if they didn't want to.

Many anarchists believe that a lot of what we see as laziness is just people being forced into work that doesn't suit their interests or abilities and is designed to make

work would include much more than today. housework and childcare are work

profit for someone else. These anarchists believe that people who are unwilling to work, or not very able, should still have access to everything they need to maintain themselves. Most people want to cooperate and want the respect and admiration of others. It is these wants that would persuade those unwilling to work to think again and start contributing to the community that supports them.

Even in **capitalist** societies most people come forward willingly to help each other out in the event of a disaster. In 2005 after hurricane Katrina local people set up the Common Ground Health Clinic. They provided care and medical assistance to each other, while the American government left people in New Orleans to die. This is just one example.

Other anarchists have already had enough of the capitalist elite consuming but not producing, and don't want to support another group of freeloaders. Such anarchists argue that there should be no compulsion to work, but also no duty to provide for people who don't want to contribute. In this scenario, the community wouldn't continue to feed, clothe and house people who are able to contribute but refuse to. However, such people wouldn't be denied access to the means of making a living for themselves, they just might not be supported by the community.

Work, being voluntary in an anarchist society, would include much more than the narrowly defined paid employment we think of today. For example, housework and childcare are work. Of course, people who can't work, like children, the sick and the elderly wouldn't be expected to work (but could if they wanted to) but would be valued and supported by the community.

27 What about people who aren't able to speak for themselves, because of age, illness or disability?

There are presently a number of people who 'can't speak for themselves', and the same would be true in an anarchist society: very young children, some elderly people, people who are non-verbal, people with severe disabilities, very sick people including those in a coma. Usually, there are ways in which we can support these people having their say in how we run things together, and in having their needs met.

Those who are carers (whether family, nurses, health workers and others in their community) will know the person as an individual, what they need, and how they communicate. There will be a 'care plan' worked out by everyone involved which explains how to support each person to have their views heard and this will be regularly reviewed and updated.

Where communication is impossible or extremely difficult (e.g. someone in a coma), family and carers can advocate for the person, drawing on their care plan and their knowledge of the person as an individual.

In present society, carers generally try and do this in the face of all kinds of obstructions. In an anarchist society their community would be actively wanting to support and help these processes happen.

There could also be huge advances in medicine and technology in the future that give us ways of communicating that we can't even imagine at the moment.

If I had a hammer...
I'd SMASH Patriarchy!!

I FOUND IT!!

CLASS STRUGGLE

15

28 What about identity politics? What if different groups feel their rights are in conflict? How would conflict and discord be dealt with?

Presently people are often discriminated against because of their **identities** (sexuality, race, religion, gender and others). In any future society, anyone facing such discrimination should be supported and encouraged to stand up for themselves, and know they have everyone else's support. An anarchist society would encourage and celebrate differences.

Presently, different identities or groups are frequently played off against each other – often claiming one is more important than the other - even though both are discriminated against. Both discriminated groups need support. Any "infighting" between groups is great for the rich and powerful.

And, the rich and powerful often encourage this infighting, so we fight each other, rather than them.

Sometimes conflicts between different oppressed groups get overheated to the point of being nearly unresolvable. But often, over time, these conflicts reduce and cool down and hopefully allowing us to work through our differences. This is often when we see there is a greater enemy (the state, police, media, judges, etc.). Presently, even anarchists sometimes get caught up in these differences.

Conflicts will still happen in an anarchist society. So we need to work on recognising and minimising them all the time. One example that comes from the recent uprising in **Rojava** (Kurdish controlled part of Syria), is the practice of 'Tekmil'. In Tekmil those being challenged listen to the comments without response. In return these concerns are only aired once - to avoid 'mob mentality'.

As we have said before in this booklet, we anarchists don't have all the answers. But as we progress together, we will learn from both our successes and mistakes. We will adapt our ways of dealing with problems and conflict and become better at dealing with all the difficult situations that arise.

16

see glossary near the back of the booklet for meaning of words in bold

29 Do anarchists believe in free speech?

Anarchists are working for a society based on people freely organising themselves, where working together is key. But anarchists don't imagine an end point, rather a continuous evolution. Nor do we imagine that all conflicts of interest or opinion will disappear in an anarchist society. It can only work if there's a constant free exchange of opinions and ideas and also a willingness to learn from collective mistakes!

So ideally speech should be free. However, in our current society we have dominant voices that often want to use their freedom of speech to abuse people or groups who have much less opportunity to reply.

Until everyone has an equal opportunity to be heard, speech isn't equal, and until it's equal it also can't be free.

until speech is equal, it can't be free

see glossary near the back of the booklet for meaning of words in bold

Some would still defend free speech in the here and now because "sticks and stones may break my bones, but words can never hurt me"! They would also argue if people are prevented from expressing their views, then open discussion is impossible. But most anarchists would disagree. In extreme cases, like present day **fascists** promoting hate speech and race violence, most anarchists would agree that this needs to be challenged, and with **direct action** if needed.

But where you draw this line is a difficult decision. It's also a difficult discussion, and although it's one anarchists won't shy away from, it will be a continual discussion and opinions may vary. It's how we deal with these differing views that is important. Communities will need to continually look at their approaches to this.

So a wide range of views, but one thing all anarchists agree with is never to ask the **state** to control or ban speech - we need to deal with it from the bottom up.

30 Would religion have a place in an anarchist society?

Most anarchists don't have religious beliefs. Indeed, the very idea of a god as the ultimate authority is a total contradiction to most anarchists. Anarchism is about people moving towards freedom and organising together. Religion is about submitting to the will of the relevant god - doing what you're told.

Anarchists are not planning to lock anyone up for having religious beliefs, or packing them off to be "re-educated". Nor are they planning to give religions special rights or powers. Religion would be seen as a matter for the individual.

Presently, most churches or religions have self appointed "leaders" who claim to speak for their whole community or religion. And these religious leaders do their best to force their members to do what they claim their particular god, priest or master says is right, without questioning. As long as this doesn't happen – and everyone is free to worship (or not worship) any god they want to – anarchists would say we should each choose what we do or don't believe in.

However, it does seem strange to us that anyone would want to let a god or gods, priest, master or anyone else tell them what to do or think on the one hand while being free to make their own choices on the other.

18

education should be broad, lifelong, non-hierarchical and voluntary

31 Would children and young people have a say in deciding how society is run?

In short, yes. In an anarchist society, children and young people would absolutely have a say in how society is run, with their input into society being valued equally to everyone else's.

Arguably schools presently function, in part, to teach the dominant "rules" of society, reproduce inequality and maintain present **hierarchies**, through, for example, standardised testing that dramatically favours the already privileged. Education is a really important part of keeping the current system going by teaching young people all the expectations and ideas needed to keep making new generations of good little **capitalists**. Despite this **authoritarian** education system many teenagers have historically participated in society by raising their voices and resisting the system through various forms of protest.

In an anarchist society, the views of its younger members would be equally important as those of adults. Everyone would work together to organise a society in which all views were taken into consideration and acted upon. For example, we could develop communal forms of education that do not attempt to indoctrinate our children and teenagers. Instead, education would exist as **non-hierarchical** spaces where children and young people voluntarily attend as free thinkers, with their ideas on how to re imagine society being taken seriously. Knowledge would no longer be received by young people from adults, but would be mutually exchanged between both, uncovering new knowledge in the process.

This means treating children and teenagers not as adults (and expecting them to take on all those responsibilities), but as equal members of society whose contributions and perspectives are valued specifically because they are young. This is just one of the ways in which we could imagine children and young people having a say in how society is run.

32 How would education work?

We wouldn't have the present **authoritarian**, top down schooling that prepares us to be good workers for the benefit of the rich and **capitalism**. We suggest people would want to learn practical skills, critical thinking, problem solving, and social skills as much as Latin, science or algebra.

Education would have some general guidelines. It should be broad, lifelong, **non-hierarchical**, diverse, person centred, and voluntary.

LEARNING ISN'T A MEANS TO AN END. NEVER STOP LEARNING!!
PAPER DOESN'T DEFINE.

People learn at different levels, so it would seem unlikely everyone in a class would be the same age. This would be encouraged to break down generational divides but also so we can learn anything at any time in our lives.

The idea you learn "x" at age "y" to do job "z" years later seems strange to us. Anarchists think many people would dip in and out of education (and work as well) throughout their lives. Others may have a specific interest and decide they want to learn more about that subject for years, which is also fine.

We don't agree with a **hierarchy** of subject matter. Maths isn't more important than (say) art or humanities or brick laying.

There would probably be limited exams, tests or qualifications with people assessed only where necessary. But, these qualifications would never be the end of learning - just milestones on a journey.

It's likely some specialist education and training would still be needed

for some people, for example, surgeons, gas fitters etc. But this would be open to anyone. Some education may need dedicated buildings and equipment. But generally anarchists feel education doesn't have to be in a building specifically set aside for "learning". But if the community decided it did, who attended and when would be decided between those running the session and those attending. Those leading it would commit to be there but anyone could attend as many of the sessions as they wished.

19

see glossary near the back of the booklet for meaning of words in bold

33 How would you deal with the climate and environmental crises?

An anarchist society would tend to create an economy with more small and medium sized workplaces, which would be more connected to local communities and ecosystems. We would see workplaces, homes and communal spaces moving over to green sources of energy much faster than presently.

Decentralisation (doing things locally) would mean people can more easily see, understand and so genuinely control technology. No longer would there be a need to under or over-produce, as production would be for people's needs not corporate greed. Alongside this, **collective decision making** within communities should lead to better ecological solutions being chosen.

The end of consumerism and the money system would mean the disappearance of all those industries like advertising which contribute towards the destruction of the environment and try to make us buy more things we don't need. Under anarchism this would lead to the end of over-production and the removal of unnecessary products (like fifty different types of washing powder).

We would also build things to last. Present society builds things that purposely break, wear out too soon or can't be repaired. Computers and mobile phones are obvious (but by no means the only) examples. This is done so **capitalism** can sell us more stuff and make more profits. But it means a massive waste of natural resources and goods get thrown away. Plus, all the power needed to produce them and the huge number of hours used. Hours we could spend doing productive work, or just relaxing.

Capitalism is destroying your mind and the planet

Present society relies hugely on private motor vehicles and the use of road, sea and air haulage to transport goods around the world. Under anarchism we would vastly increase public transport and environmentally sustainable ways of getting people and goods around. We would also produce goods more locally.

All homes would be effectively insulated and we would move from using fossil fuels to more environmental energies like solar, wind and water power.

just imagine how much further we could get using open source science in our communities

34 Would anarchists ban scientific research and technology development?

Scientific knowledge is knowledge of the physical world based on evidence from observation rather than on opinion, faith or wishful thinking. We need to understand how physical processes work so we can feed and shelter ourselves, prevent disease and tackle climate change.

When scientific knowledge is developed in secret, for the purposes of making profit or gaining power, we often get technologies which harm us rather than improve our lives. For example, the drive for profit and control means that artificial intelligence is being developed by governments, the military, and private companies, for weaponry, surveillance, or to manipulate us to buy products or support certain causes. Our own devices, identities and data are used, without our knowledge or consent, and we have less and less control over the technology which affects us.

In an anarchist society, science, like everything else, would be supported by the agreement of the whole community, on the basis that it provides public benefit. It would be open source (without secrecy or ownership of ideas and freely available to all) allowing the community to monitor its ethics, risks and benefits. Science would be an activity carried out in workplaces and education. Private labs in competition with each other wouldn't exist. Without the drive for profit, the scientific community could concentrate on sustainable food production, energy and transport, healthcare and more.

Advances could be shared to solve global problems. For example, manufacturing instructions for a new vaccines would be available so that the vaccine could be made

21

anywhere, not just by one company selling it at inflated prices, unaffordable to poor communities.

Just imagine how much further we could get using open source science in our communities. We could design systems for efficient democratic decision making, fair distribution of resources, and really start tackling global challenges together.

people would live in whatever way they wanted so they are safe, happy and encouraged to think for themselves

35 Would we still have nuclear families in an anarchist society?

The simple answer is "yes, if people want to live that way". A **nuclear family** traditionally refers to a husband, wife and children. One principle anarchists agree on is everyone should be allowed to do what they want as long as it doesn't harm others.

Everyone should be able to live in the way that suits them best. With the "family" this can be extended families living together; groups of people bringing up children together; people deciding they don't want children; same sex couples with or without kids. Or any other combination that works for those individuals - including the nuclear family.

But, it would need to work for everyone within that "family". Often in present society the nuclear family works for the father but may not be good for the mother or the children. If it works properly for all involved, then go for it. If it doesn't, all those involved can discuss ways of making it an enjoyable way of living for all of them. Society would support them to try to make it work better. If it still doesn't work, those involved should feel confident to look at different ways of living.

Likewise, if any other "family" set up needed support they should get it. If their way of living wasn't working for all of them, they should all be able to try different ways.

People would live in whatever way they wanted so they are safe, happy and encouraged to think for themselves. And none of us should judge how other people live, or judge them if they try loads of different ways of living.

Hopefully in an anarchist society all of us will be mixing with a range of other people, getting experiences and knowledge from a number of places – not from just within one particular arrangement.

36   Would drugs be allowed? What about alcohol and tobacco?

In an anarchist society we would expect the number of people using drugs (including alcohol and tobacco) to reduce as time went on, as people wouldn't have such difficult lives. There would also be less reason to make a habit of it. So they would be mainly for relaxation.

Even so, drugs may affect the user's health, and could have impacts on other members of society. Does that give "the community" the right to ban them? Most anarchists would stress the individual's ownership of their own body. A **dictatorship** of public

anarchists stress the individual's ownership of their own body

opinion is still a dictatorship! It would be up to each community to discuss and agree on the broader question of the balance between the individual and the community.

In an anarchist society we would ask who would produce these items? Coca growers in Latin America, opium growers in Afghanistan and monks brewing the Buckfast wine favoured by many alcoholics do it because it gives them the best income. Heroin and cocaine are no different from fish fingers, veggie burgers - or weapons - in that respect. Kenyan coffee growers switched to crops they could eat when the bottom dropped out of the market - and were much healthier! We suspect far less would be produced as communities started growing/ producing more useful crops for themselves.

Perhaps individuals would brew/ grow their own favourites. Maybe the broader society would decide to do it **collectively**? This would be part of the wider question of what, in an anarchist society, we would decide to produce.

37 Would media/ social media be regulated?

At present, most major media companies want to make money (through advertising revenue or selling user data). They also want to spread ideas (frequently to gain some political influence) by drawing in more and more people. Also, as long as there are things to be outraged about, media outlets will exploit our emotional responses to them. So we need

people's ability to connect globally will finally fulfil its promise as a force for good

see glossary near the back of the booklet for meaning of words in bold

to be mindful about allowing ourselves to be exploited.

Capitalist society is based on competition, image, and selfishness. Social media is an exaggerated version of that.

We believe that in a future anarchist society people would be respectful of others. Guidelines, agreed collectively by each community, should be in place so that all of us know what is considered appropriate or not.

As for the technology itself, it is difficult to know how that will change in the future.

We'd like to think people's ability to connect globally will finally fulfil its promise as a force for good, and encourage other people to consider a different form of society.

38 What will happen to fashion, art, music, culture, entertainment, fun?

"If I can't dance, it's not my revolution" Emma Goldman, anarchist, 1869 - 1940

It will continue as it always has, evolving with the times and the tastes of the people who are creating it. People will have more time to explore their creative side and produce whatever weird and wonderful works their imagination allows.

"if I can't dance, it's not my revolution" Emma Goldman, anarchist, 1869 - 1940

It wouldn't be like it is in today's **capitalist** society where artists' works are pushed upon us by others who will benefit financially from their success.

There are many talented people out there today whose work is never recognised and often lost as a result. Many carry on because they have a passion for what they are creating and enjoy it, even though they can't make a living out of it.

People want to entertain and be entertained. We all like different things and this adds to the richness of life. We will never have a shortage of amazing art.

We think an anarchist society will enable more individuals to enjoy being creative in a huge variety of ways. Isn't this the point of it all? Living and doing what you love, and for many, that's some form of creative activity.

see glossary near the back of the booklet for meaning of words in bold

HOW DO WE GET FROM HERE TO THERE?

23

see glossary near the back of the booklet for meaning of words in bold

39   But don't we need political parties and leaders to be able to make changes?

We do not need political parties and leaders to make a better society - they are standing in our way!

The way present society is organised makes it easy to assume we can't make changes without getting governments to pass laws or provide the money for something to happen. For example, people campaigning against laws banning abortion or homosexuality decided to focus on getting political parties in government to change the laws. Instead we could have focussed on making the bans unworkable, as queer and trans people did in the US's legendary **Stonewall riot**.

As the Covid epidemic spread, workers took action to protect themselves, without waiting for politicians. The rapid spread of **mutual aid** support groups throughout the country also showed people were organising

to protect themselves. Ordinary people reacted long before politicians did. When society is organised in an anarchist way we will make the changes we need directly.

In the meantime, there are many examples of people taking direct control and making changes. Two are; after the Tottenham riots (2011), and the Grenfell Tower fire (2017). In both cases local people **self-organised** to provide **solidarity**, support and mutual aid to those in need. There are many other examples we could use as well.

The movement for community food growing has increased massively in recent years, as people take over land to provide what they need. Self-organisation of workers is also often directly responsible for change. NHS staff were the ones who coped with Covid and organised a successful vaccine roll-out despite mismanagement by government. After Word War 2, mass **direct action** by those who had sacrificed so much in the war brought improvements to working people's lives. One example was returning soldiers occupying empty army bases for places to live. Such actions were part of the general movement that led to social housing and other improvements.

people with wealth and power aren't just going to give it up

40 Shouldn't we gradually reform what we have rather than changing everything?

It all depends what you actually want to change!

If you just want more middle class jobs and the things that you can buy for yourself then you don't want revolution. You want a chance to be better off than most people in the world, to join those that exploit you. At a certain point hopefully you'll realise you're on a losing ticket. A system that's built on some people getting rich at the expense of the majority can't easily be turned into one where we all aim to cooperate and everyone can get what they need.

For anarchists the fundamental question is "who has the power?". A system that's built on a few people having the real power won't gently change into one where everyone has it. That's because those with the wealth and power

aren't just going to give it up. They might feel forced to make some reforms if they feel threatened, but this is the opposite of giving power. It's people using the power they have to stay at the top of the pile. Leopards don't change their spots.

As anarchists, we want people to run their own lives, cooperating with each other not just in our own neighbourhood, but ultimately across the world. At the end of the day we're not asking the **state**, government or the rich and powerful to do anything for us. They will always act in the interests of the **ruling class** they are a part of. We want everyone else to join together and do it ourselves.

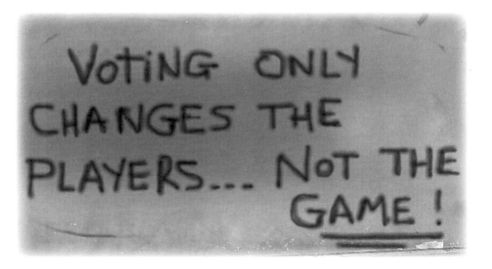

41 What is this direct action you lot talk about?

Definitions of direct action include "something done as the most immediate way of achieving an aim" and "a form of political activism, in which participants act directly, ignoring established political (and industrial) procedures."

Examples include political graffiti, strikes, workplace occupations, demonstrations, sit-ins, **sabotage**, squatting or revolutionary guerrilla warfare. Most anarchists would not include demonstrations. Sabotage is when people deliberately obstruct, damage, or destroy something for political advantage. This could be people occupying or destroying something like an arms factory or a coal burning power station. But it can simply be one fed-up worker literally "putting a spanner in the works" to disrupt production.

Some people use the term direct action for what anarchists would see as little more than radical

24

see glossary near the back of the booklet for meaning of words in bold

lobbying. Here the action is appealing to a government to change a particular policy, rather than the people involved in the action actually changing something themselves.

Often those doing the radical lobbying intend to get arrested and state their case in court. This is sometimes called "Speaking Truth to Power". Most anarchists believe those in power already know the truth.

For anarchists a fundamental issue is that direct action should increase the confidence of all those carrying it out. That's only possible if everyone has a genuinely equal say.

For anarchists committed to **class struggle**, any proper revolution has to be organised mainly by poor and **working class** people. So any direct action is only justified if it gives them a sense of power - even if they're not directly involved in it.

42 Would a revolution be violent? Wouldn't governments suppress any attempts at real change with force?

The media usually portrays anarchists as violent and destructive and most people imagine an anarchist revolution would be the same. This is a misunderstanding of anarchism.

An anarchist revolution is not a revolution that topples one group of rulers to replace them with another – such revolutions often are violent but don't really change things. An anarchist revolution would transform how society works by changing how decisions are made. Rather than one event, it will be a process, where people increasingly realise that they don't have to put up with things the way they are and that they themselves can organise society in a freer, fairer way.

Such a process might start by people organising themselves locally, taking over their workplaces and running them for the benefit of themselves and their community, rather than the benefit of bosses and shareholders. They might also start taking over providing services to the community.

There have been many examples of workers running their own factories and of people organising community services for themselves. Examples include the 800 community health centres, municipal clinics and hospitals set up by the **Zapatista** movement of local people in Mexico which run to this day. Or, the Argentinian workers who in their thousands, from the early 2000's, re-opened factories closed by their owners and ran them **collectively**.

Of course, if such activity starts to gain ground, it's likely to be challenged by the **state**, or by individuals keen to turn situations to their own advantage. In such cases, people have defended what they have gained, by force where necessary.

Anarchist ideas are seen as dangerous by those who benefit from the existing system, and there are likely to be violent attempts to suppress them if they are seen to be gaining ground. However, the greater the proportion of people who refuse to accept being exploited, the greater the chance that the existing order can be replaced, with less bloodshed, by something far better.

the revolutionary process is essentially a creative one

see glossary near the back of the booklet for meaning of words in bold

43 How do we know a revolution won't end in chaos and destruction?

The current system is seriously flawed in so many ways, that if humanity is even going to survive, it has to be overthrown. As the **capitalist** ruling class will not give up their power willingly, then a revolution is necessary.

Not all revolutions are successful. The **Russian Revolution** is a prime example.

Nevertheless, there are many things we can do to ensure that a revolution will lead to a much better society rather than chaos and destruction. Firstly, we begin

if humanity is going to survive, the current system has to be overthrown

to create the new society in the shell of the old. In other words, we now begin the process of developing the structures and practices of **non-hierarchical self-organisation**. Malatesta, an Italian anarchist (1853 - 1932), had much to say about the importance of organisation. Whether it be our own political organisations, a **housing co-op**, a union, or a community garden, we can gain experience in running things for ourselves effectively and without **hierarchies**.

Secondly, we need to begin to bring people together on a number of levels - locally, nationally and internationally. The more people get used to working and organising together the better placed we will be to create a well organised new society that will be global.

In addition, the less violent the revolution the better. Malatesta also had something to say about that. He argued that the bigger the revolutionary movement, the more people involved, the less there will be a need for violence. This will make it easier for us to continue the process of making our vision a reality.

44 Why would anyone support some sort of revolution when the outcome is unknown?

A revolution is not a one-off event in which society changes completely from one way of working to another. The change will be the result of a process that will have been on-going for many years, involving all of us creating a vision and the conditions for a new society. What we do now - the actions we take and the structures we create - will shape the kind of society we end up with. Therefore, although we don't have the exact format for a new society, the outcome won't be completely unknown.

However, it's important to recognise that we can't foresee exactly what will happen. There is indeed some risk the revolution won't lead to the society we want. This is why it's important to develop a vision and begin to create "the new society in the shell of the old".

We do expect and encourage new ideas to emerge as a result of the revolutionary process, which is essentially a creative one.

25

see glossary near the back of the booklet for meaning of words in bold

Once people are freed from the constraints of the present society, they will be able to imagine and put into practice new ways of doing things that haven't been thought of before. There is an element of the unknown. But it will be us who are making new things happen - they won't be imposed on us.

The revolution is also necessary. We may not know exactly what will happen but we know that what we presently have can't go on. Issues like climate change and the extreme injustices of **capitalism** (and other **hierarchies**) mean that we feel we have no choice but to work towards a complete break with the current society.

we want a better society by convincing others to be part of it - not by forcing them

45 What would happen to people who opposed an anarchist revolution?

When people ask this question they often seem to think that anarchists would shoot everyone who oppose us; just like the rulers did in the so-called **Communist** states or as present day **dictators** and some **capitalist** leaders do. It certainly isn't the way anarchists work!

Also, we don't see the "revolution" as a big one-off thing – it will be fairly gradual over many years.

But to answer the question, it would really depend on how anyone opposed the revolution.

If those that didn't like our ideas started using repressive violence, then naturally the anarchists and those agreeing with them would fight to win!

But, if people who didn't like the revolution were opposing it in other ways: say by discussing what they saw as a better way forward or handing out leaflets suggesting a different way - then that's totally within their rights and they should do that without any fear. We believe our views are the best there presently are, but we want a better society by convincing others to be part of it - not by forcing them to do what we say is best.

We want people involved because they think it's the best way to live. We are fine with people challenging us and suggesting different ways- even **hierarchical** ways! Although we see no sense in having a society where a tiny minority boss the vast majority of us around. Why would anyone want that?!

46 Isn't it "human nature" to compete with others to get the best for us and our families?

It would be very weird if we didn't want the best for ourselves, our families, friends, and those we personally care about. Anarchists are not alone in believing we don't have to "compete with"- i.e. trample on - everyone else to get it.

There is increasing evidence, and more people, that question if human nature was ever actually

26

competitive or selfish. When humans were first evolving there were small numbers of them and resources were plentiful, so there was no need for people to be selfish. This is still seen in groups that continue to live as they did in those hunter gatherer times. So if we are selfish, it's a recent development and certainly not 'human nature'.

Anarchists believe the vast majority of us would be better off if we all cooperated. Everyone competing with each other keeps us divided and only benefits the rich. Even in this **capitalist** society when workers stand together and fight they're a lot better off than when they're isolated individuals grovelling to the boss for a few extra crumbs. And this benefit from working together will become much larger as that cooperation spreads.

Before the UK introduced a welfare state run by the **ruling class**, workers ran their own medical **friendly societies** (they employed the doctors!). Even in Chile, under the military dictatorship, workers formed **mutual aid** projects. And there are factory and land occupations across the world.

The challenge for anarchists is to help sustain projects where cooperation among ordinary people is already happening, prevent the **state** from undermining or replacing them, and work to increase them. And also resist the increasing attacks by those with most to lose from real change.

there is increasing evidence that questions if human nature was ever selfish

47 Don't most people want an easy life and are happy for others to make decisions?

A lot of people may just want an easy life, but what we know is that people live in and react to the environment around them. Most of the people we know have grown up in a world where they have been stripped of their ability to make decisions for themselves. From schools that demand a respect for authority without question, to the governments which make decisions that suit themselves regardless of how much people object. We are taught that our opinions do not matter, and we shouldn't question the way the world is - it just is. Get on with it and enjoy all the opportunities and pleasures that life has provided you with.

This is the world we know, and it can be easy to draw the conclusion that this is what people want. But this is not the only way life can be organised. There are societies around the world where people

there are societies where people actively participate in decision making as a part of daily life

THERE'S NEVER MONEY TO FEED THE POOR BUT ALWAYS PLENTY TO FIGHT A WAR

see glossary near the back of the booklet for meaning of words in bold

actively participate in decision making processes as a part of daily life for example:

- Indigenous communities
- Assorted libertarian zones of the past, for example, in **Spain 1936** or **Manchuria 1930**
- The **Zapatistas**, or **Rojava**, in our own time.

And it happens here in the UK too. We see people collectively organise together to solve issues, time and time again. The distribution of **mutual aid** support groups during the COVID crisis, and the **Friendly Societies** in days gone by, are good examples. We know that a lot of people have this spark in them, and that the possibility of a world where we all take responsibility can exist.

hoarding money will begin to be pointless

48 How do we get the rich to give up their wealth?

Presently it's difficult to get anyone to reduce their living standards in favour of a fair distribution of resources, especially if they are unsure of the future. Many speeches, books, social media posts etc. have clearly described the evils of inequality. But still the rich get richer and more powerful.

As said before, an anarchist society won't happen instantly. As society's ideas change some wealthier individuals will see there is more to life than increasing their wealth. Building communities, getting rid of individual greed, sharing all resources and seeing the benefits for all of a fairer society, will gradually convince many richer people that they don't need huge amounts of stuff and wealth.

As we move nearer to an anarchist society, the **state** will gradually disappear, hoarding money will begin to be pointless and all resources, like raw materials, workplaces and land, will start to come under community ownership.

Everyone will have an equal say in decision making and free access to everything produced by society.

Some might try and cling onto their wealth. But under anarchism, these people will no longer own the resources that provide them with the wealth they have under **capitalism**. Without money and our labour they will no longer increase their riches by investment. Without the state there will be no schemes designed to funnel money upwards via the public purse from poor to rich. Without the politicians, police, judges and the army no one will protect them and their wealth.

But even after all this, if they still try and hoard while others have less, then each community will decide what they feel is fair. Communities may let them have more. Or communities may convince them to give up their excesses. Or communities may well just go and redistribute what the wealthy are hoarding. If necessary at the point of a gun.

in the end power cannot lay in the hands of a tiny minority and has to be shared

see glossary near the back of the booklet for meaning of words in bold

49 What about power? How do we get them to share that?

Anarchists believe there are two kinds of power. One is power over other people. The other is our own individual and **collective** power to run our own lives. In an anarchist society nobody will have power over others.

As we advance towards an anarchist society, we can hope powerful people will see the advantages of a free and **cooperative** life. But we suspect many may not.

Whether it's being a **dictator** or someone inflicting domestic violence, being able to force other people to do what you want can be very addictive. The process of revolution will erode that power, as people experience taking control of their own lives, but many power-addicts will fight tooth and nail to retain it.

In an anarchist society, it's not simply about being able to do whatever you like, so anyone refusing to give up their power will probably need to be confronted by the rest of their community.

How each community does this, as we have said before, depends on the specific circumstances. We have given some examples how it could happen, but communities will develop others as well.

But, in the end power cannot lay in the hands of a tiny minority, it has to be shared between us all.

yes, we do think an anarchist revolution can start on a smaller scale and then grow

50 Does the revolution need to happen globally or can it happen on a smaller scale?

Ideally the anarchist revolution would happen globally. Obviously cooperation between different parts of the world would be easier, with all national borders abolished.

But we are realists and know this may not happen globally at the same time. It's more likely to start on a smaller scale at first.

Currently there are anarchists and sympathisers throughout the world. One way it might happen is if anarchist practices start becoming dominant in one area. This would hopefully lead to anarchism and anarchist ideas taking root more widely. This could then start to develop in most other countries, as anarchists there feel more empowered, and others are won over to anarchism.

Some **states** are more oppressive than others, have different economic and social conditions and different amounts and types of political culture. This means the revolution is likely to develop at different speeds.

Anarchists don't believe in money So if anarchism only started in one or two areas how would they trade? This would be decided at the time but here are some ideas. The revolution might cover a wide enough scale that there's enough of everything we need within the

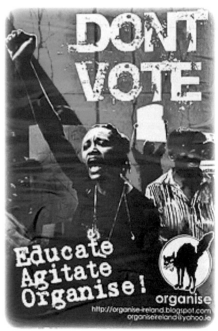

see glossary near the back of the booklet for meaning of words in bold

revolutionary space. We might decide to go without something that we don't really need. We might barter with less revolutionary areas. Maybe we compromise and sell stuff we produce to other places and use that money to buy things we need within the liberated areas. Or use money seized from the banks!

It's difficult to say for certain how or if trade would happen. Many factors will come into play, which we can't even guess at here. But yes, we do think an anarchist revolution can start on a smaller scale and then grow. Be great though if it did happen worldwide all at once!

51 Can we really change things?

The simple answer is 'Yes we can'. If we couldn't, society would be the same as it's always been and it definitely is not. We got rid of the divine right of Kings; the church's power is much reduced; and many barbaric customs have gone. Things we take for granted, like paid holidays or weekends, were not given to us by generous employers but fought for by previous generations. Recent years have seen these gains eroded, with laws limiting strikes and giving employers more power. But workers in new **grassroots trade unions** are fighting back and winning significant victories.

Examples exist in other areas. Women have achieved huge advances towards equal treatment in society (but not enough). People with disabilities have fought and won victories for themselves. These reforms are far short of what anarchists want. That requires **capitalism** and the **state** to be replaced by a society based on anarchist principles.

Two examples many anarchists see of this are in **Spain** during their Civil war and the self-ruling indigenous community of Cheran, Michoacan, Mexico.

THE PEOPLE DON'T KNOW THEIR TRUE POWER

In 2011, led by local women, the people of Cheran rose up to defend their forest from armed loggers and kicked out corrupt police and politicians at the same time. Political parties are banned. Using **direct democracy** everyone gets a say and decisions are made by **consensus**, from who will get a local job in construction, to the allocation of public services.

During the Spanish Civil War in 1936, groups organised along anarchist lines operated the factories, mills, docks, transport, shops and utilities without managers or the state. Peasants took collective control of the land. In many areas money was abolished. These groups created economic equality based on need and ability. It was a shining example of how things could be.

29

52 So ask yourself, what kind of future do I want to see for myself and the world?

An anarchist society would be a fairer, equal, more democratic society.

A **non-hierarchical** system, where everyone has a say in how society is run.

a society in which people can follow their dreams...

Where decisions are made that benefit the local community and wider society, without the need to consider company profit margins or the corrupt self-interest of politicians and wealthy individuals.

Millions of people would be freed from the jobs that offer no benefit to society, like the financial sector.

A society in which no one goes hungry and where everyone has access to the medicines they need and the best health care. Where people can follow their dreams, get the education they want, find meaningful, interesting work and travel or settle wherever they like without barriers or restrictions.

Once the power has been taken from the few, we can work together to address the problems that exist in our communities and globally without the obstacles that prevent real change.

... find meaningful, interesting work and settle wherever they like

Glossary

Accountable / Accountability
This means having to answer for your actions and decisions to others connected to you such as workmates, neighbours, etc.

Anarchy. Literally means 'without power' - from the Greek, without ('An') power or authority ('archy'). Anarchism is the belief that everyone should live without any power over others.

Assemblies. Also known as People's Assemblies, these are the basic level of organising in a non-hierarchical system. They are open to everyone and are the group that makes decisions. Discussions about how the group operates are decided in a group meeting or assembly (could be face-to-face or using technology). Everybody in that area or workplace is welcome and has an equal say in running things and the workload is shared.

Authoritarian socialists/ communists. See "state run socialism".

Capitalism. The system we live under now. Capitalism is an economic, political, educational, social and cultural system in which a few own and control property to benefit their own interests. A society of bosses, profits, landlords, etc. and the division between rich and poor.

Class / working class / ruling class. There are lots of different definitions of class, but very broadly it describes the split into 2 classes - the ruling class with power, wealth and connections and the working class who only have their labour to sell to make a living and only have the power they can generate through mutual aid and solidarity with the rest of their class.

Class struggle. Refers to the constant and wide ranging conflict between the working class/ exploited and the ruling class/ exploiters. Almost everyone is in the first group even though some still work for or identify with the interests of the ruling class or own a relatively small amount of property or wealth.

Collectives/Collectively. A group of people working together towards a common goal and generally making decisions by some agreed form of consensus decision making.

Communism (communists). A way of organising in which all property and resources are owned by the community and each person contributes according to their ability and receives according to their needs. However, over the years its meaning has been corrupted and those in power or the media purposely mistake it with "state run socialism" (see state run socialism).

Conflict resolution. See "mediation"

Consensus or consensus decision making. Here, instead of just voting, a group discusses an issue and tries to get everyone within that discussion or group to come to an agreement. This sometimes takes longer and people need to be more flexible, either by being prepared to compromise or by looking for different answers. Getting everyone to agree isn't always possible or practical, so over the years guidelines have developed to help groups decide on what to do when consensus isn't reached. See - www. seedsforchange.org.uk/consensus

- as a starting point. Many communities around the world decide things this way. And many international trade agreements are agreed this way. It's just those in power love to con us that voting is the only way – as it benefits the powerful.

Cooperatives (e.g. workers and housing). A co-op is an organisation that's owned and controlled by its members, to meet their shared needs. The members can be workers, residents or anyone who has a say in how the co-op is run. In a worker's co-op the workplace is run equally by everyone (and we do mean everyone) who works there. It could also, if people wanted, include people from the local area. In a housing co-op a number of homes (say all the homes in a street or estate) are again run equally by everyone who lives there.

Decentralisation. Capitalist states are centralised. Here the greatest power is held in the centre, often by one person (a president or prime minister). In Non-hierarchical systems power is held by assemblies and so is decentralised.

Delegates. People sent by an assembly to larger meetings to truly represent people. They are given instructions by their assemblies to do specific things, so are not put in a position of exercising power themselves. Delegates can be instantly recalled (the assembly that sent them can replace them) which stops them saying something different to their assemblies' views.

Dictatorship. A form of government which is characterised by a leader, or a group of leaders, which holds governmental powers with few to no limitations.

Direct democracy. Everyone has the power to make decisions themselves (in assemblies) rather than passing this power to politicians in elections (which is indirect or representative democracy).

Factory committees. See "workers' councils"

Fascism. Far-right, authoritarian, ultra-nationalist, racist and violent political belief. Fascists believe in a single all powerful dictatorial leader, using force to strictly control every aspect of society

Friendly societies. These were workers' self-help mutual aid organisations. The first began around 1500. By the time they were effectively replaced by the authoritarian hierarchy of the welfare state they were providing everything from insurance against temporary unemployment to GPs and hospitals for their members.

Grassroots Trades Unions. The International Workers of the World, Cleaners & Allied Independent Workers Union, and United Voices of the World are three of these. These were set up by workers wanting to control their own struggles instead of being controlled, and sold out, by mainstream trade unions.

Hierarchy - see non-hierarchical

Identity politics. A political approach wherein people of a particular race, nationality, religion, sex, gender, sexual orientation, or other identifying factor develop political agendas that are based upon these identities. Identity politics is connected with the idea that some groups in society are oppressed and begins with analysis of that oppression.

Justice - Reparative. Here the "offender" compensates their victim by covering losses resulting from the crime, either with money and/or services.

Justice – Restorative. This both tries to restore the victim and community to their pre-crime conditions, but goes a step further. Alleged offenders are encouraged to admit their guilt and try to atone for it.

Justice – Transformative. This aims to transform those involved for the better. It attempts to change society as a whole as well as the individuals involved. It tries to give victims answers to why they were victimised. It also requires the offender to work to change themselves, usually with the assistance of others.

Libertarian. The opposite of authoritarian. The definition we use here is that It doesn't mean people can do whatever they want, but that no one is forced to do anything and all decisions are made by everyone having an equal say. Others use different definitions.

Manchuria's Anarchist zone. This was in what is now North East China. It lasted from 1929 to 1931. The zone included shops where everything was free. Worker and peasant cooperatives and free education were set up throughout the zone, along with Regional assemblies.

Mediation and conflict resolution. This is where trained people try and help others who can't agree on something to agree on the issue. Mediation tends to be where individuals or groups work out the best way to go forward so that everyone is happy. Conflict resolution tends to happen when individuals or groups are more agitated with each other. On a small level it could be helping people in a group come to a decision they all can accept. On a larger level it could be stopping wars by mediation between the two sides. Both these happen in present society. In an anarchist society more of us would have the access to this help and also be trained to help others.

Mutual aid. Helping and supporting each other based on need and expecting nothing in return.

Nationalism. A belief that demands loyalty, devotion, or allegiance to a nation or nation-state. It also believes that such demands outweigh other individual or group interests, particularly class. It is often a base for emerging racism or fascism. Anarchists want a society without nationalism.

Non-hierarchical. This is where there is no leader, president or manager type role and no inferior ones either. Instead members of a group, organisation or collective all have an equal say in how the group is run, what the goals are and how to reach those goals. A hierarchy is any relationship that is unequal. We live in many hierarchies. Some are obvious such as having politicians and bosses in charge, and some less obvious, such as some people being confident and listened to because of their gender or class background. Anarchists are against all hierarchies.

Nuclear families. Traditionally refers to a husband, wife and children, where the male is the dominant person.

Participatory democracy. See "self-organisation".

Paris Commune. This lasted for 2 months in 1871. After driving out the French Army, the citizens of Paris declared Paris an independent commune. All elected on the Central Council were instantly recallable and got the average worker's wage. Policies expressed the immediate needs of the working class. Workers took over enterprises deserted by their owners. Rent was cancelled, police and child labour abolished and the Catholic Church made powerless. The French Army returned in overwhelming force and the insurrection was crushed.

Recallable delegates. See "delegates".

Representative democracies. Casting a vote every 4 or 5 years after which you have no further say in any decision making, and the so-called elected leaders then do whatever they want.

Rojava 2012 to present. Rojava (in the Kurdish controlled part of north and east Syria) has tried to implement a number of anarchist ideas. It strives for gender equality and tolerance of all races, religions, and political views without hierarchies. Some elements of the revolution are organised along anarchist lines and demonstrate that this is possible in the modern world. This has been achieved while Rojava is involved in armed conflict against ISIS, Syria and Turkey and is faced with a severe embargo.

Ruling Class. See "Class"

Russian Revolution. Although this started with a lot of local organisation - some anarchists in Russia in 1917 saw the "soviets" much like we today see our assemblies – the Communist party quickly destroyed the non-hierarchical "bottom up" approach and brought in a strictly hierarchical "top-down" approach including excessive violence against anyone who objected.

Sabotage. To deliberately obstruct, damage, or destroy (something), for political and economic advantage. Sabot, where the word sabotage comes from, was the name of wooden clogs worn by French workers and which they used as a tool to destroy machines.

Scarcity - the difference between how much of something is needed and how much is made available.

Self-organisation. Another way of describing non-hierarchical organising, because people decide what happens themselves without external or higher forces telling them what to do. Horizontal is another word used to describe the opposite of hierarchies. Another similar phrase is Participatory democracy because everyone is involved all the time, rather than simply casting a vote every few years as in our current representative democracies.

Solidarity. Helping and supporting each other based on need and expecting nothing in return.

Soviets. See "workers' councils"

Spain 1936. There was a workers' revolution that began at the outbreak of the Spanish Civil War in 1936 and for two to three years resulted in the widespread implementation of anarchist and, more broadly, libertarian socialist organisational principles throughout various parts of the country. In Barcelona in particular the anarcho-syndicalist CNT trade union (run by its members) took over, and very efficiently ran everything from factories to public transport to the telephone exchange. Out in the countryside people went a step further, collectivised the land, and abolished money.

State. A country's governments, parliaments, monarchies and all the agencies, flags, borders that go with them plus an expectation that everything is done via them. The state also runs or regulates education, culture, health services, media, religions, municipals and the market, to a certain extent, and maintains control with forces like police, courts, prisons, military and spy networks.

State run socialism. This describes countries such as China, the Soviet Union, Cuba and many others that called themselves socialist or communist but operate with a very powerful government which controls every aspect of life and economy. Authoritarian socialists/communists are those that defend and intend to create similar systems (although they might claim to want to do things differently).

Stonewall Riots. Also called the Stonewall Uprising, began on June 28, 1969 when New York City police raided the Stonewall Inn, a gay club located in Greenwich village. The raid sparked a riot among those in the bar and neighbourhood residents as police attacked employees and customers. This led to six days of protests and violent clashes with cops outside the bar, in neighbouring streets and in nearby Christopher Park. The Stonewall Riots kick started the gay rights movement in the United States and around the world.

Ukraine 1917-21. Anarchist Nestor Makhno and his comrades launched an anarchist army in 1917 as peasants took over the land. Makhno and his supporters attempted to reorganise social and economic life along anarchist lines, including setting up communes on large private estates, the redistribution of land and the organisation of free elections to local soviets (councils) and regional congresses. At the same time a spontaneous wave of peasant land occupations spread across Russia from February 1917 onwards.

Workers' councils, soviets, factory committees/groups. These are some of the different types of organisation that bring together people in their workplaces and communities. They are similar to "assemblies" mentioned above.

Working Class. See "class"

Zapatistas. The Zapatista Army of National Liberation went "public" with their short lived New Year's day 1994 armed takeover of 7 cities in Mexico's Chiapas region- rejecting the US/Mexico Free Trade Agreement (NAFTA). Following this local people expelled landowners from their estates, abolished private property and established autonomous communities. These survive to this day, in spite of intermittent conflict with the Mexican state. Largely self- sufficient, they operate workers co-ops, family farms, community stores and universal healthcare, while pushing strongly for women's equality. As with Rojava, there are different views around what the relationship between the armed wing and the actual communities really is. They have consistently reached out to other grassroots movements including those outside Mexico with their international "encuentros"/assemblies.

Image Credits

Further Reading

What follows is a selection of books and websites that inspired a load of us to become anarchists or want to find out more about this inspirational view that ordinary people can organise society and all its bits and pieces much better than politicians.

A lot of these books have been digitally copied and made free on the internet. Places to start looking for them could be

https://theanarchistlibrary.org

https://libcom.org/library/

If you buy the books don't use Amazon or some other dodgy supplier. Support Anarchist shops and distributors. Some we know of are:

AK Press
www.akuk.com

Freedom Bookshop
www.freedompress.org.uk

PM Press:
http://www.pmpress.org

Active Distribution
www.activedistributionshop.org

Some other website that are worth visiting are:

Anarchist Frequently Asked Questions:
http://anarchism.pageabode.com/afaq/index.html

A Infos
http://www.ainfos.ca

Reading List

Colin Ward
Anarchy in Action
180 pages 1973
With chapters on the family, schools, housing, crime, employment, welfare, deviancy, planning, and more, this is probably the best practical example of anarchist ideas in action. As he writes in his introduction, "This book is not intended for people who had spent a lifetime pondering the problems of anarchism, but for those who either had no idea of what the word implied or knew exactly what it implied and rejected it, considering that it had no relevance for the modern world".

Alexander Berkman
ABC of Anarchism
145 pages 1929
Berkman was born in 1870 under Tsarist dictatorship, emigrated to the US and was jailed for fourteen years after shooting an industrialist whose thugs had opened fire on striking workers. This book by one of the most gifted writers for the anarchist movement answers some of the charges made against it and presents the case for communist anarchism clearly and intelligently. Thorough and well stated, it is today regarded as a classic statement of the cause's goals and methods.

Peter Gelderloos
Anarchy Works
281 pages 2016
Gelderloos takes examples from around the world, picking through history and anthropology, showing that people have, in different ways and at different times, demonstrated mutual aid, self-organization, autonomy, horizontal decision making, and so forth--the principles that anarchy is founded on--regardless of whether they called themselves anarchists or not. This is an inspiring answer to the people who say that anarchists

are utopian: a point-by-point introduction to how anarchy can and has actually worked.

Lorenzo Kom'boa Ervin
Anarchism and The Black Revolution and Other Essays
2013
From Lorenzo "I wish to introduce young people and especially Black people and other people of color to revolutionary Anarchist ideals. This book will discuss Anarchism and its relevance to Black and Third World liberation movements...My views are not necessarily those of any group, although I speak generally of the theories of Black Autonomy, an ideological tendency within the Anarchist movement. It is up to the reader to determine whether these ideas are valid and worthy of adoption."

Errico Malatesta
At the Café
160 pages 1920
In 1897, while Malatesta was hiding from the police, he regularly went to a cafe in Ancona, Italy. This wasn't an anarchist cafe, but had a variety of customers including the local policeman. The conversations he had in this cafe became the basis for the dialogues that make

up this book. Malatesta, in his usual common-sense and matter-of-fact style, sets out and critically analyses the arguments for and against anarchism. This is a classic defence of anarchism, that anticipates the rise of nationalism, fascism and communism.

Simon Read
Everything You Wanted To Know About Anarchism But Were Afraid To Ask
60 pages 1985
An excellent, short introduction to anarchism, its ideas, and some of the thornier issues in life ("don't we need the police to catch criminals," "aren't people naturally selfish," "don't we need some kind of management," etc).

Marcos Mayer
Anarchism for Beginners
170 pages 2003
Commercial book about anarchist ideas with many illustrations. Maybe not the best but an easy read to get a basic idea of anarchism.

Emma Goldman
Anarchism and other essays
280 pages 1910
Anarchist and feminist Emma Goldman is one of the towering figures in global radicalism of the late 19th and early 20th centuries. An early advocate of birth control and women's rights, as well as a dedicated anarchist, she was an important and influential figure in such far-flung events as the Russian Revolution and the Spanish Civil War. In addition to her classic essay which lays out anarchist ideals, this volume contains six other essays on prisons to marriage, direct action, violence, and sexuality.

Stuart Christie and Albert Meltzer
Floodgates of Anarchy
140 pages 1970
This book looks at anarchism in relation to class struggle. It presents an argument against class-based society and hierarchy and advocates for a free and equal society based on individual dignity and merit. It argues that the state/government is the true enemy of the people and that only through the dissolution of government can the people put an end to exploitation and war, leading to a fully free society.

Clifford Harper
Anarchy A Graphic Guide
212 pages 1987
A clearly written and simple introduction to anarchism, beautifully illustrated in Clifford Harper's distinctive woodcut-style, published in 1987. "Like all really good ideas, Anarchy is pretty simple when you get down to it- human beings are at their very best when they are living free of authority, deciding things among themselves rather than being ordered about." So begins this anarchist classic.

Cindy Milstein
Anarchism and Its Aspirations
140 pages 2010
Cindy provides an overview of the history and hopeful future for a better world. It quickly brings even the uninitiated reader up to speed with a crash course on some of the most influential anarchists in history and their ideas on how we might achieve the transformation of society. It looks at how these principles have been put into practice by groups such as the Situationist International, social ecologists, Zapatistas, anti-globalization activists, and other directly democratic organizations and communities in their respective struggles against capitalism and state control.

Anarchist Federation
Introduction to Anarchist Communism
40 pages 2015
Anarchist communism is an economic and political system based upon removing oppressive and exploitative structures in society (such as capitalism and the state), and building a society where everyone has an equal input into decisions that affect their life. This pamphlet sets out a short introduction to Anarchist Communism.

Chaz Bufe
A Future Worth Living
Thoughts On Getting There
26 pages 1998
This pamphlet briefly looks at why things are the way they are, why people put up with it, why both anarchism and Marxism have failed, and what we can do about it—principles, practices, and projects that could lead to a "future worth living."